The Reflection

Melissa Hause

BookLeaf Publishing

Presentation by *BookLeaf Publishing*

Web: www.bookleafpub.com

E-mail: info@bookleafpub.com

ISBN: 9789395756525

First edition 2022

DEDICATION

I would like to dedicate this book to my husband Braun and daughter Violet. Braun is my biggest support to all my creative projects. Violet's smiles and giggles help me to not take life too seriously and learn more about being true to myself and going outside my comfort zone. I would also like to dedicate this book to all my family and friends who have made the chapters of my life a story to tell!

ACKNOWLEDGEMENT

I would like to acknowledge BookLeaf Publishing for putting out the 21 Day Writing Challenge!

PREFACE

"They value every single thing, that you have come through.
Think of all the very things you have to write,
Through all the ups and all the downs that you see in sight." Knowing that through your mistakes you learn and grow and make edits to keep trying to be the best version you can be. Every day is a page in the chapters of the story that you write. You need to believe in the story of you!

A Mindful Reflection

Accept yourself for who you are now,
Negative thoughts you will not allow.
Never so perfect, only so real,
Knowing this feeling is okay to feel.
Turning your weakness into a strength,
Then you can go any way or length.
Always working better to be,
Knowing you are the best that you see.
Know in your mind and inside your heart,
This is only the beginning, only the start.
Things always changing in this world that we
live,
Making sure kindness and compassion we give.
Be kind to your neighbours, be kind to your
friends,
Being kind to yourself, let the kindness not end.
Love yourself the way you are,
No need to change one little scar.
Value yourself in the brightest light,
Hold on to that with all of your might.
Everything happens, know just for a reason,
That we will be going through each changing
season.
Lucky to have all that you do,
Knowing it will help to get you right through.
To yourself, always be kind and always be fair,

Know in your heart you will always be there.
How lucky you are to have people with you,
Those you can count on and get you on through.
But to realize they need me too in their life,
Through all the good times and bad times of
strife.
Helping others by just being you,
Knowing they're learning everything too.
Making sure to not criticize,
See the best things within your eyes.
Just a chapter, not the whole book,
Learning from it will help you look.
Everyone's different, and that is okay,
Knowing your heart in every way.
Take care of yourself and then you will see,
All in life that you were meant to be.
Know that you are so very unique,
Qualities others are willing to seek.
Things that are the best for you,
Balancing goals, working on through.
Not putting down others along the way,
But helping them step up and having a say.
Know you are human, know as you are,
You are allowed to shine like a star.
Show everything that you have come through,
Know to be the best version of you!

Flowing Thoughts

The rain falls down the window glass,
Waiting for the time to pass,
Listening to the words of the song,
Knowing you can face things however wrong.
Lot's to do in these next weeks,
Ideas and knowledge my brain seeks.
Time to write, time to read,
Inspiration I will need.
Learning so much from this year,
So much out there less to fear.
Putting it together, what I know,
Final papers ready to go.
Hoping the sun will come back,
Reading my essay I get on track.
I scribble down what I learned,
To the next page I then turned.
Knowing exactly what I want to say,
Beginning to be a beautiful day.

The Need to Belong

Belonging is how you'll befriend,
Your friends of yours who'll lend.
Acceptance of others you will show,
As a member, a part of how you grow.
Belonging is a human need,
Those you are with, who help you succeed.
In your behaviour will be aware,
To act within norms that you truly care.
Understand how one acts,
And how others will react.
Belonging is when you begin to start,
Somewhere you are, who you're a part.
Predicting how others will respond,
Will determine where you belong.
Conflict exists that you create,
Behaviour to resolve will motivate.
Self-regulation is a core,
Of where you belong, what you're looking for.

We All Belong

What makes us all belong? Is it we're the same?
Or are we very different, the feelings thoughts
that came.
We all think very different; we all know
different things,
Opinions, answers, questions and the songs we
sing.
What makes people dislike us so, what will be
the end?
What makes us different could be your very
friend.
We all belong here on earth, don't you think one
bit,
That just because your different that that could
be it.
Know deep inside your heart, people love you,
They value every single thing that you have
come through.
Think of all the very things you have to write,
Through all the ups and all the downs that you
see in sight.
Make sure your very voice is the one that's
heard,
For you could be the very one of which a disease
is cured.

Just remember we all belong, and diverse, it's so,
Believe in your thoughts and feelings, and in
your heart though.
We have the power to shine through, this is
really true,
Just know being different will/can get you
through.

Praxis

When I sit and read a book, I cannot see clear,
I sit, reflect and think about what is really near.
I imagine things are different around this very
world.
I sit here thinking irrelevant things and my hair I
twirled.
Maybe it's time to read in depth, and the things I
write.
Will soon in time give me another shining light,
Praxis is combined thinking then to do,
I read the book then once more all the way
through.
I get to the end, then reflect, thinking less of me,
Getting out in this world and to really see.
Experience is what you will get,
After sitting an reflect.
Always know you can't sit back,
So your doing will not lack.
People in the world will show,
And your knowledge will further grow.

Relief

Too much stress, too much worry,
In my hand my face I burry.
Thinking things are the worst they can be,
Gotta stay strong, for others and me.
Even when you think things are rough,
Feeling like you've dealt with enough.
Don't give up it's the worst you can do,
Having hope and pushing on through.
Thinking things are the worst they can be,
I look back on it all re-evaluate and see.
The negative is just all in my head,
Looking at a different perspective instead.
Just wanted people by my side,
Inside of me these feelings I hide.
Wanting to talk about my troubles and fears,
Letting out all of my tears.
Thinking things are the worst they can be,
Cause this is not a dream it's the reality.
I blast my music and run to unwind,
Feeling relieved to have cleared my mind.
Now it seems like all a relief,
Just have faith and keep your belief.

Stigma

What is all the stigma around?
All these thoughts that people found.
People might not understand,
Others want to lend a hand.
Sometimes you will want to talk,
Others want their mind to block.
Sometimes you can feel quite sad,
Feelings like you've never had.
Nevermind what people say,
Up you get to start your day.
Some things said not always true,
Just please know to be your "you".
Read and learn and you can teach,
Then new heights you will reach.
Then the answers you will find,
In your heart and in your mind.
Let's just focus how to treat,
And in the end you will beat.

The Reflexive Self

Interact with people in lots of various ways,
The approach and attitude on these different
days.
This is my reflexive self, this is what I do,
How I will react and the behaviour I choose.
Sometimes it's spontaneous, sometimes well
thought out,
Sometime I will talk my thoughts, or sometimes
I will shout.
Thinking is important before you do speak,
Even if your having a kind of hard week.
People will react to their own friends,
A message within that your voice sends.
Attitude is important to show,
It is through this people will know.

It All Matters

How we see a different race,
Seeing the world from a different place.
How we see a different age,
Seeing the world at a different stage.
How we see a different class,
Seeing the world at a different mass.
Look at yourself to have the power,
and view the world at every hour.
Constructing knowledge and a view,
Influential as a writer too.
Intelligent in a different way,
Learning things every day.
It all matters how we see,
A bright future which will be.

New Knowledge

It's not what is said but what is not,
with a good memory I sat down and thought.
Every day I learn something new,
new experiences and information too.
Everyone is smart in their own very way,
maybe it will be clear someday.
My music block out all the people around,
but very much aware, I watched and found.
The way people are treated is not always fair,
Some acknowledged, others "not there".
Some people will truly understand,
they are the one's who'll lend a hand.
Others just bystanders on the street,
some on the curb with nothing to eat.
Some privileged and go to school,
other's hanging in the streets so cool.
You find something new every day,
lots of people with things to say.
Not always what you want to hear,
some people you may even fear.
Stand strong and believe in what you know,
you have many places in this world to go.

Motivation

How one knows to motivate,
To initiate their lively state.
Features of an action; drives, goals and needs,
Moving and intensity and persistence leads.
Intrinsic motivation, doing a job you love,
Something you are good at and what you think
of.
In our perceptions it is that we live,
Plan, reflect, self-regulate and in time you'll
give.
Knowing to move on and progress can be made,
So your doubts and fears will and soon can fade.
What motivates behaviour is optimism and hope,
Always know that feeling will always help you
cope.
Instead of being critical, foster self-esteem,
Then it is in your life you will find your dream.

Believe

Believe that there is something more,
Out in the world you're looking for.
Something so significantly mere,
Something you will hold onto dear.
Knowing people who are on your side,
People you trust and those you confide.
When you cry and when you mope,
These friends of yours will help you cope.
Can't catch your breath and need some air,
They'll be the ones who truly do care.
The past shapes you and who you are now,
Negative thoughts you will not allow.
Believe you're the best you can truly be,
Don't give up and you will see.

Imagine

Thinking to myself, unsure of the way,
Imagine going back to the day.
The day that if just went all wrong,
Not knowing, where you would belong.
A peaceful world that we would make,
Friendships' of others we would not take.
Being friends of others together,
Even through the stormy weather.
Not leaving them to fend on their own,
Making them feel like their all alone.
Stopping the violence visible or not,
This is just an imaginable thought.
Trying to not cry myself to sleep,
My pillow soaked with the tears I weep.
Hopefully people will start to be nice,
Not thinking about it more than twice.
This world could be more than good,
If people did the things they should.
Trying so hard to make things right,
In the future a better sight.
Just imagine all of this,
The things that people often miss.
Making clear to others so new,
So they will see the pathway too.

Perspective

No one ever thinks the same,
It all just seems like such a game.
Guessing about what goes through one's mind,
Not in the present but in the future you'll find.
The answers to everything you wanted to know,
Some things should be left to fulfill and grow.
Not everything can be our own way,
Others also have things to say.
No one care, or that's how it seems,
In real life or in my dreams.
Where ever I go nothing is real,
I'm not exactly sure how to feel.
Who can I trust and who will I not?
That's up to me; I'll decide what I want.
Put trust into those who'll not deceive,
Only those who'll help you believe.
Sometimes you just need some space,
Some time to think in your own little place.
A time to just clear your head,
By leaving the past behind instead.
This is just a perspective of things,
The path uncertain in this life brings.

Empathy

Perspective of another you'll understand,
Understand the feeling you'll lend a hand.
Lend a hand and you'll do good,
Doing good like you always would.
Always would from their place,
From their place, hard times you'll face.
You'll face what is new to you,
New to you, you will get through.
Getting through the way you feel,
The wat you feel will help you heal.
Helping you heal is how you think,
How you think is how your mind links.
Your mind links and you will find,
Finding thoughts in your mind.
Your mind thinks of how to increase,
Increase positive acts piece by piece.
Piece by piece perspective of another,
Perspective of another you will uncover.

Mirrors

Mirrors do not, always show through,
The inside of the person looking at you.
Just a surface reflecting back,
The beauty you see, not what you lack.
There are many things a mirror can hide,
Not showing those who have lied.
Some act the part of who they are,
Doing this won't get them far.
When you look at yourself in the mirror,
Not liking the image, you'll shed a tear.
A broken mirror shattered to the ground,
With a smashing, clashing, crashing sound.
The looking-glass self is what people see,
Trying to fix it, change and be free.
No more labels, no more fear,
A foggy mirror is not always clear.
Being who people want you to be,
Finally realizing, that's just not me.
They set a label, you play a role,
That's not how you will reach your goal.
Always know the reflection inside,
Is not the one you're wanting to hide.
Know who you are so very true,
Believe in the hope and a future so new.

The Reflection

Words I regret, "Do you want to be my friend?"
Thinking this friendship would come not to an
end.
We were like sisters, so very much the same,
Dressing like twins, but then the day came.

We were not as similar as I had once thought,
I followed too much and said not a lot.
Acting as though I didn't exist,
I didn't see, there was much I had missed.

We started fighting all the time,
Things just turned on a dime.
Nothing important I would express,
And holding in all my distress.

Coming home to let out my tears,
Trying to forget all of my fears.
Going to school and getting put down,
Thinking she wore the golden crown.

To my other best friend I could never talk,
She thought I was mad, wouldn't go for a walk.
I wanted to fix it, but it was too late,
For these troubling years would soon be my fate.

They ganged up on me, three against one,
Certainly nothing could ever be done.
Telling the teacher what I had to say,
replying, "Just a phase, it'll be okay".

No one ever really got,
How this anger gave me thought.
Dismissing every "little thing",
Hoping a good life soon would bring.

Now before I said, "I regret",
But really I can never forget.
Was this to happen all for good?
That things will end up as they should?

My friends all taken away from me,
What did I do? Can this all be?
Didn't know till nine years time,
How things in this life would soon be fine.

The reason people would never believe,
                    Is because she had another trick
up her sleeve.
Ruining everyday and causing much pain
Thinking I was the one so very much insane.

Destroying every good thing in one's life,
Was her very main goal and causing such strife.

Emotionally abusive all these years,
Hiding this from all other peers.

It's all covert and no one can see,
Or feeling this pain as much as me.
It's only at school that the troubles arise,
But not only there do tears fill my eyes.

All of my friends soon caught the drift,
So happy how my life would now shift.
I was no longer alone and confined,
This future was finally now to be mine.

No longer listening to rules not my own,
So much to say and in mind I have grown.
I am myself and no one else can decide,
take away goals or knowledge inside.

Control is what they only want,
Being correct and to weak ones they taunt.
They show no care or empathy too,
This is how they are, what they will always do.

Making you upset and making you cry,
To them it's okay but you wonder why?
Is everyday what I really deserve,
How can they honestly have so much nerve?

You look back and say is it all real?

That's never how you intended to feel.
Maybe I need to start to be tough,
I have surely taken more than enough.

Standing up for what I really believe,
Making the decision to finally leave.
Putting up no more with this type of act,
It really is a truthful fact.

I have friends that stand by me,
And a mother supportive as can be.
No more reflecting what I see,
Being true to myself is the key.

Decisions

So many things in this life to decide,
Sometimes feelings you're wanting to hide.
Unsure of yourself and what you should do,
Doubting your thoughts and not following
through.
Just be yourself and you will see,
Certain things are not meant to be.
Stressing little about the past,
Holding true those things that will last.
Knowing those who are on your side,
Friends of yours you turn to confide.
In the end it'll always show,
Whose friendships' meant to fulfill and grow.
Then you'll have the answer to take,
And know which kinds of decisions to make.

It Just Takes One

Resilience to see the light,
That growing up will be alright.
In hard times it'll get me through,
Reaching out is what to do.
When I feel so very weak,
School is where I often seek.
In the pages of a book,
Freedom comes where I look.
Survival skills and smarts of the street,
Help my journey to defeat.
Making an effort to connect,
So I boost my intellect.
Being so collaborative,
It's my best that I will give.
Wanting to reach a potential so full,
To get out of the push and pull.
It only really truly takes one,
So something significant can be done.

Under the Surface

25

Nobody can really see,
Underneath the surface of me.
Quiet, shy and nothing to say,
Those who don't know me will see it this way.
Opinions, ideas, I have a voice,
To those I tell I have a choice.
I understand people and what they can do,
I observe, watch and see right through.
Dishonest, uncaring and telling of lies,
Blind to some, but not my eyes.
Look deep inside past the surface,
And you will see that person's purpose.
Figure out those so untrue,
In a new light people you'll view.

Your Life

Meaning of this is what you'll define,
Nobody else's or even mine.
Confused for a while,
Your frustrations will pile.
You make the final say,
Of where you're going every day.
What path you lead, which road you take,
Even all the friends you'll make.
You have a voice and decisions so true,
No one else can control you.
Being assertive and very strong,
Finally find where you belong.
Endless possibilities, it's not over yet,
So much further in this life to get.